TYRANNOSAURUS REX

AND OTHER FEROCIOUS PREDATORS FROM THE MESOZOIC ERA

JACQUELINE BALL

becker&mayer!

CONTENTS

THE MESOZOIC ERA

HUNTERS AND THE HUNTED

Animal life started small. Some of the earliest creatures were no bigger than a grain of sand. Over millions of years, life grew . . . and grew . . . and grew. Colossal reptiles roamed the land and filled the seas and skies. Some were hunters. Others were their prey. It was the Mesozoic Era, the age of the dinosaurs.

The Mesozoic Era lasted 185 million years. Scientists divide it into three geologic time periods: Triassic, Jurassic, and Cretaceous.

EORAPTOR

TRIASSIC
251–200 million years ago

In the Triassic period, all the land was in one supercontinent called Pangaea, which was surrounded by ocean. The climate was hot and dry. Small dinosaurs such as *Eoraptor* [EE-oh-rap-ter] shared the planet with flying and swimming reptiles, fish, insects, spiders, and mouse-size mammals. The top hunters were massive crocodilians, which lived both on land and in the sea.

PANGAEA

Eurasia

North America

South America

Africa

Tethys Ocean

India

Australia

Antarctica

251–200 MILLION YEARS AGO

 STAURIKOSAURUS

 COELOPHYSIS

 PROCOMPSOGNATHUS

 RIOJASAURUS

 SALTOPUS

 PLATEOSAURUS

200–145 MILLION YEARS AGO

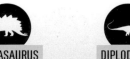 STEGASAURUS

 DIPLODOCUS

 CERATOSAURUS

 ARCHAEOPTERYX

TRIASSIC

JURASSIC

JURASSIC
200–145 million years ago

The Triassic period ended with a mass extinction. The supercontinent of Pangaea split into two chunks, Laurasia and Gondwana, with a shallow sea in between. The climate became wet and warm. The first birds appeared. Dinosaurs grew to massive sizes. Meat-eating dinosaurs moved up to the top of the food chain, with *Allosaurus* [AL-oh-SORE-us] at the peak in North America.

ALLOSAURUS

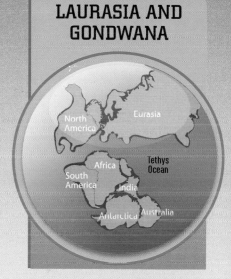

LAURASIA AND GONDWANA

CRETACEOUS
145–65 million years ago

By the Cretaceous period, Laurasia and Gondwana had broken into multiple continents. The climate was warmer. The seas were higher. There was no ice at the North or South Poles.

Dinosaurs became the biggest they would ever be. Some plant eaters grew to massive sizes, with long, long necks. Others sported spectacular frills, crests, and armor. Regardless of size or shape, in North America at the end of the period, they were all fair game for *Tyrannosaurus rex*, the "King of the Cretaceous."

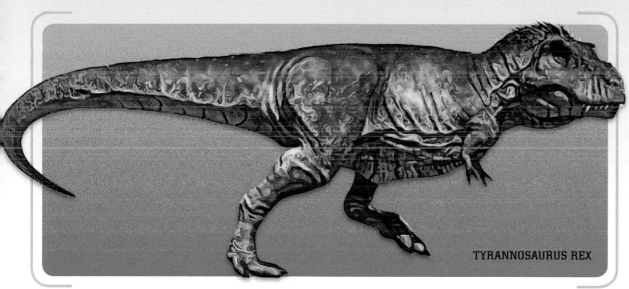

TYRANNOSAURUS REX

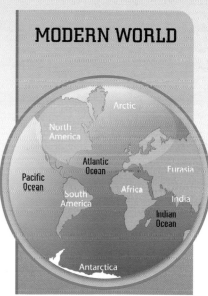

MODERN WORLD

KNOW WHAT?
Dinosaurs survived for 160 million years. Humans have been around for less than one million years.

145–65 MILLION YEARS AGO

 IGUANODON

 ARGENTINOSAURUS

 OVIRAPTOR

 VELOCIRAPTOR

 PACHYCEPHALOUSAURUS

 ANKYLOSAURUS

 TRICERATOPS

CRETACEOUS

BORN TO KILL

Animals that hunt and kill other animals are predators. The animals they catch and eat are their prey. Most predators hunt alone, but wolves and certain other hunters form a pack to surround and overpower large prey.

In the natural world, predators kill for only one reason: to survive. They are not being cruel or evil. They are simply following nature's number one rule: every living creature has to eat. Of course, that doesn't make natural predators any less terrifying—especially to their prey.

KEEPING LIFE IN BALANCE

Different types of animals eat different things.

TYRANNOSAURUS REX

Carnivores
eat other animals.

TRICERATOPS

Herbivores
eat plants.

EORAPTOR

Omnivores
eat plants and other animals.

CARNIVORE: TYRANNOSAURUS REX	OMNIVORE: EORAPTOR	HERBIVORE: TRICERATOPS	PLANTS	INSECTS	EGGS

Carnivores claim the top of the food chain. Without meat eaters, populations of herbivores would grow too large and eventually die out. Without plant eaters, vegetation would overrun the earth. Every living thing plays an important role in keeping life in balance.

REPTILES RULED

During the Mesozoic Era, reptiles ruled as the top predators. There is a special term for these dominant reptiles: *archosaurs* [ARK-oh-sores]. Mammals would not rise to the top spot, which they hold today, until the next era.

Sea Predators

Gigantic *plesiosaurs* [PLEE-see-oh-sores] dominated the seas. One of the most powerful, *Liopleurodon* [lie-oh-PLUR-oh-don], prowled for prey in deep water, guided by its strong sense of smell. Experts say *Liopleurodon*'s massive jaws were powerful enough to bite through a car.

Flying Predators

Colossal *pterosaurs* [TAIR-oh-sores] such as *Quetzalcoatlus* [KETZ-uhl-coe-AT-lus] soared over the plains of North America. This spectacular reptile was one of the largest flying animals of all time, as tall as a giraffe and with wings wider than a small plane. *Quetzalcoatlus* had no teeth, but it could easily eat small dinosaurs after scooping them up in its massive jaws.

Land Predators

In the early part of the Mesozoic Era, one of the biggest land predators was *Postosuchus* [post-oh-SOO-kuss], an enormous prehistoric crocodile that walked on four legs and had a mouth full of daggerlike teeth. Dinosaurs were about the size of adult humans at the time—small enough to be snack food for *Postosuchus*. By the end of the era, dinosaurs would evolve to include immense meat eaters, including the one and only *Tyrannosaurus rex*.

TYRANNOSAURUS REX

TYRANT LIZARD KING

Tyrannosaurus rex comes from Greek and Latin words meaning "Tyrant Lizard King." The name perfectly fits the biggest meat-eating dinosaur in North America during the late Mesozoic Era. *T. rex* reigned over all other creatures in its time and place.

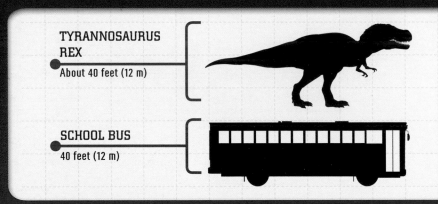

TYRANNOSAURUS REX
About 40 feet (12 m)

SCHOOL BUS
40 feet (12 m)

AMERICAN IDOL

Tyrannosaurus rex is North America's very own dinosaur. Every *T. rex* fossil found so far has come from the western part of the continent, in a wide strip going south from Canada to Texas. But *T. rex* is a rock star all over the world.

Tyrannosaurus rex wasn't simply a predator. It was an apex predator. That's an animal that has no natural predators within its ecosystem. Polar bears, African lions, wolves, and sharks are all modern apex predators. The only killers any of them have to worry about are humans. But humans weren't around in *T. rex*'s world. No other living creature threatened the tyrant king's throne.

FAST FACT

Three or four 12-year-olds standing on each other's shoulders would almost reach *T. rex*'s hip.

OPEN WI-I-I-DE

How did *T. rex* hold on to the top predator spot for millions of years? It took full advantage of its deadly built-in predator tools.

JAWS AND TEETH

T. rex's skull was as big as a refrigerator. The gigantic head held four-foot (1 m) long jaws that could snap shut with more force than any animal that ever lived.

The jaw contained 60 spiked, saw-edged, banana-shaped teeth that were hard as rocks. Powered by the immense force of the jaws, the teeth could smash through skin and flesh to crush bone. <u>*T. rex* could rip off a 500-pound (227 kg) slab of flesh in one bite</u>.

Scientists say *T. rex* did not chew its food. To turn prey into a meal, the teeth in different parts of its mouth did different jobs. The front ones gripped and pierced to hold an animal in place. The side teeth tore flesh. The back ones chopped chunks of meat into pieces small enough to swallow.

8 INCHES
(20 CM)

500 POUNDS (227 KG) = 1 AMERICAN ALLIGATOR

4 FEET (1 M)

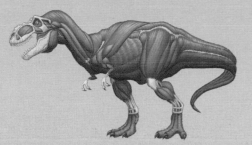

LEGS AND FEET

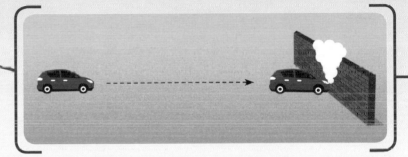

Tyrannosaurus rex had extremely strong thigh muscles and long legs. Some scientists say a young *T. rex* might have run at speeds between 15 and 25 miles per hour (24—40 kph). Older ones would have moved more slowly but still fast enough to chase down prey. (Some herbivores only moved a couple of miles per hour.)

The rear feet were enormous. Each one supported several tons. <u>When *T. rex* ran, its feet hit the ground with the force of a car slamming into a wall at 30 miles per hour (48 kph).</u> No doubt its prey could feel the vibrations from a distance, but the impact didn't necessarily slow *T. rex* down. Its feet had special padding to absorb the shock.

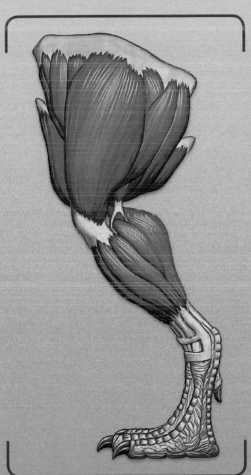

SENSES

T. rex skull fossils show eyes pointed farther forward than most other predatory dinosaurs. Scientists say that shows it had good binocular, or 3D, vision. Skull fossils also show large nasal cavities, which mean it also had an excellent sense of smell. Its nose knew when prey was around, even when it was far away. There was no hiding from *Tyrannosaurus rex*.

EDMONTOSAURUS

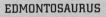

? KNOW WHAT?

T. rex preyed on plant-eating dinosaurs like *Edmontosaurus* [ed-MON-tuh-SORE-us]. *T. rex* also preyed on some of the largest dinosaurs in the world. With massive bodies to nourish and gigantic stomachs to hold and digest the tons of leaves and bushes, herbivores ate nonstop.

FAMOUS FOSSIL FINDS

We've been finding pieces of *T. rex* for well over 100 years. Fossil hunter Barnum Brown discovered the first *T. rex* skeleton in 1902, in Montana's Hell Creek Formation. Since then, amateurs and scientists have dug up about 50 *Tyrannosaurus* fossils.

BARNUM BROWN

MOVIE STAR

Scientists at the American Museum of Natural History in New York City, where Barnum Brown was a curator, constructed a *T. rex* skeleton model using the fossil Brown found. Today *Tyrannosaurus rex* towers over the museum's Hall of Saurischian Dinosaurs. The skeleton has become famous from *Night at the Museum* and other movies, books, and TV shows.

Actually, the skeleton now looming over the dinosaur hall is not the first one assembled. In the original, *T. rex* stood upright, with its tail dragging. But, by the 1990s, new scientific research showed that position was not realistic. Scientists rebuilt the skeleton to show *T. rex* in a hunting pose, with its head down and tail straight out for balance.

A NINE-TON *TYRANNOSAURUS* NAMED SUE

Another famous *T. rex* skeleton is at the Field Museum in Chicago. This one is the biggest, most complete *T. rex* skeleton ever found, measuring 42 feet (13 m) long and 12 feet (4 m) tall at the hip. Experts say this creature could have weighed nine tons (8,165 kg).

Its name is Sue, but scientists don't know if it was a male or a female. They named it after Sue Hendrickson, the paleontologist who discovered it.

KNOW WHAT?
Fossilized poop is called *coprolites*. It can tell us a lot about how prehistoric creatures lived, and especially what they ate. One of the largest coprolites ever found measured 15 inches (38 cm) and contained bits of bone from a small meat-eating dinosaur. Scientists think the coprolite may have been left by a *T. rex*.

A DEEP (AND SMELLY) DIVE INSIDE T. REX

Although fossils give us a lot of information about prehistoric creatures, they are just starting points to discover even more. Scientists use them to start new explorations of how T. rex and other prehistoric creatures lived, looked, and even how they sounded. They come up with new theories and then test their ideas with the help of modern technology.

1 T REX = 3 AFRICAN FOREST ELEPHANTS

HEAVYWEIGHT

Fossils tell us that *T. rex* was huge. But how huge, exactly? How much did this monster predator weigh? At one time most scientists would have agreed a grown *Tyrannosaurus rex* had a maximum weight of six tons (5,443 kg). Then researchers decided to make 3D computer models of five *Tyrannosaurus* skeletons of different ages, using medical scanners.

The models helped the team discover that earlier weight estimates were off—way off. Now scientists say a full-grown *T. rex* could weigh as much as *nine* tons (8,165 kg), 50 percent more than they previously thought.

SLOW DOWN

With medical scanners, scientists can create 3D images and use them to build skeletons that they can animate to show how dinosaurs moved. For *T. rex*, one team came up with a top speed of 15—25 miles per hour (24—40 kph) for a teenage dinosaur.

HEAR ME ROAR

We may never know exactly what sounds *T. rex* and other dinosaurs made, but scientists keep trying to figure it out. They are experimenting by blowing "virtual air" through the cavities in computer models made from scans of fossilized dinosaur skulls. They are also reconstructing soft tissue to come up with ideas about what sort of sounds the noses and throats may have made.

WHAT A CUT-UP

Soft tissue doesn't usually last long enough in the wild to become fossilized. Either animals eat it or it decomposes. So it's not surprising that no preserved *T. rex* has ever been found.

In 2014, scientists and movie special effects professionals decided to make their own. They teamed up to create a seven-ton (6,350 kg) model based on the latest scientific information. They used latex, foam, and plastic to create flesh, bone, and internal organs. They even made fake blood with colored corn syrup.

The model took four or five months to build—and was almost immediately cut up on TV by four scientists performing a make-believe autopsy. The scientists wanted *T. rex* to seem more real to viewers. And viewers got a really BIG show!

1. They saw a heart 100 times as big as a human heart and eyeballs the size of small melons.

2. They saw scientists use a chain saw to cut through the tough, scaly skin and flesh and into the bone.

3. They saw rings in a leg bone that showed how old the animal was, the same way rings in a tree trunk show a tree's age. (This one was a teenager.)

4. They learned that intestines are small for meat eaters like *T. rex*, but the heart and lungs are large. That's because predators need extra oxygen for the chase.

5. Luckily, viewers did not learn how stinky the inside of a dead *T. rex* could be. But they could tell from the reaction of the scientists. The horrible stench brought tears to their eyes. The special effects people had added badger poop to the stomach contents to make it extra realistic.

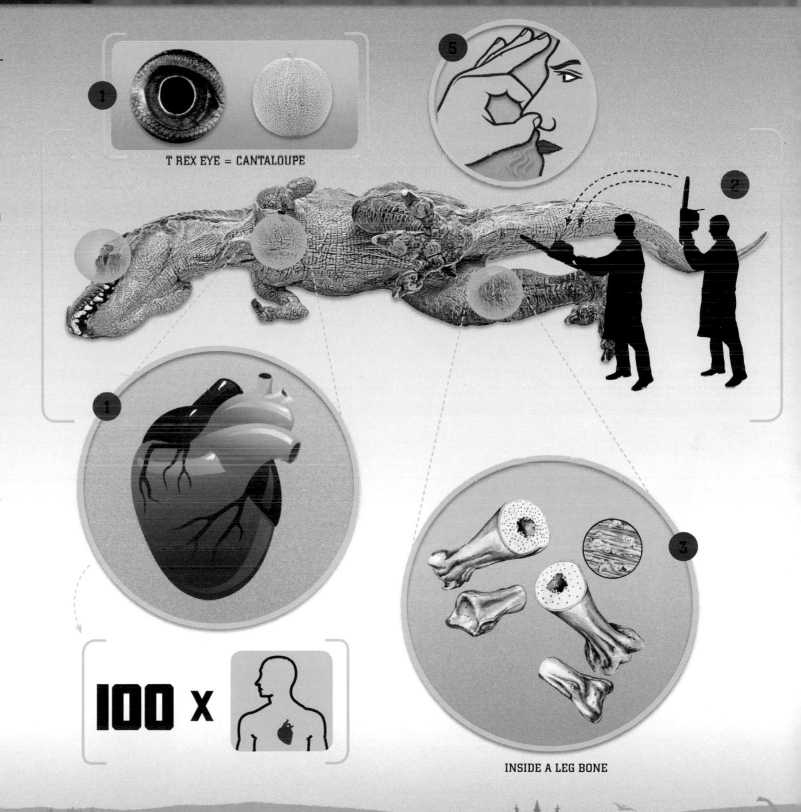

T REX EYE = CANTALOUPE

100 x

INSIDE A LEG BONE

THREE PUZZLING QUESTIONS WITH SURPRISING ANSWERS

Everything about *Tyrannosaurus rex* seems to fascinate people, but these questions are especially intriguing. The answers may surprise you. They may also change as new research comes to light.

QUESTION: What were *T. rex*'s tiny arms used for?

ANSWER: Maybe nothing.

Everyone agrees that the very short arms of *Tyrannosaurus rex* looked weird with its massive body. They were too short to reach its mouth, so they could not have been used to eat. But they were strong, with two long clawed fingers on each one. One possible explanation was that *Tyrannosaurus rex* might have dug claws into prey and tossed the unlucky animal into its gaping jaws. Another was that *T. rex* held prey in place with its arms and then swooped down for the kill with those monster jaws.

To try and answer the question with technology, researchers made a scan of a fossilized *T. rex* arm bone and used it to make a detailed 3D image. They reported seeing few signs of stress marks or indications that the arms were used frequently. So at the moment, the most popular answer is the simplest: the arms were useless.

QUESTION: Did *T. rex* have feathers?

ANSWER: Probably.

Honestly? Could this most terrifying predator of all time have been covered with feathers, like a . . . chicken? Yep, it could have happened.

Tyrannosaurus rex was a theropod, the type of dinosaur from which scientists say birds evolved. Most agree that theropods, such as raptors, were fully feathered. So it is likely that *T. rex* could have had feathers, too. Perhaps only a crest on its head or a line down its spine lasted into adulthood, but newborn *Tyrannosauruses*, needing the insulation, were most likely completely covered.

WARM-BLOODED: VULTURE

COLD-BLOODED: RATTLESNAKE

QUESTION: Was *T. rex* warm-blooded, like a mammal, or cold-blooded, like a snake?

ANSWER: Probably somewhere in between.

Cold-blooded animals can't make their own heat. They have to get it externally, from the sun. Scientists say that predatory dinosaurs such as *T. rex* were too active to waste time following the sun for energy. They had to be on the move constantly to get food.

Also, cold-blooded animals grow slowly. Scientists know that teenage *T. rexes* grew very fast. So many scientists have decided that *T. rex* was neither as warm-blooded as a mammal or bird nor as cold-blooded as a snake or crocodile. It was somewhere in between.

OR

WHAT'S FOR SUPPER, T. REX?

This is one question scientists can answer for sure. The proof is in the poop.
The crushed bones of *Edmontosaurus* and *Triceratops*, both late Cretaceous herbivores, have appeared in *T. rex* coprolites, or fossilized poop. So there you go.

T. rex prey

EDMONTOSAURUS

TRICERATOPS

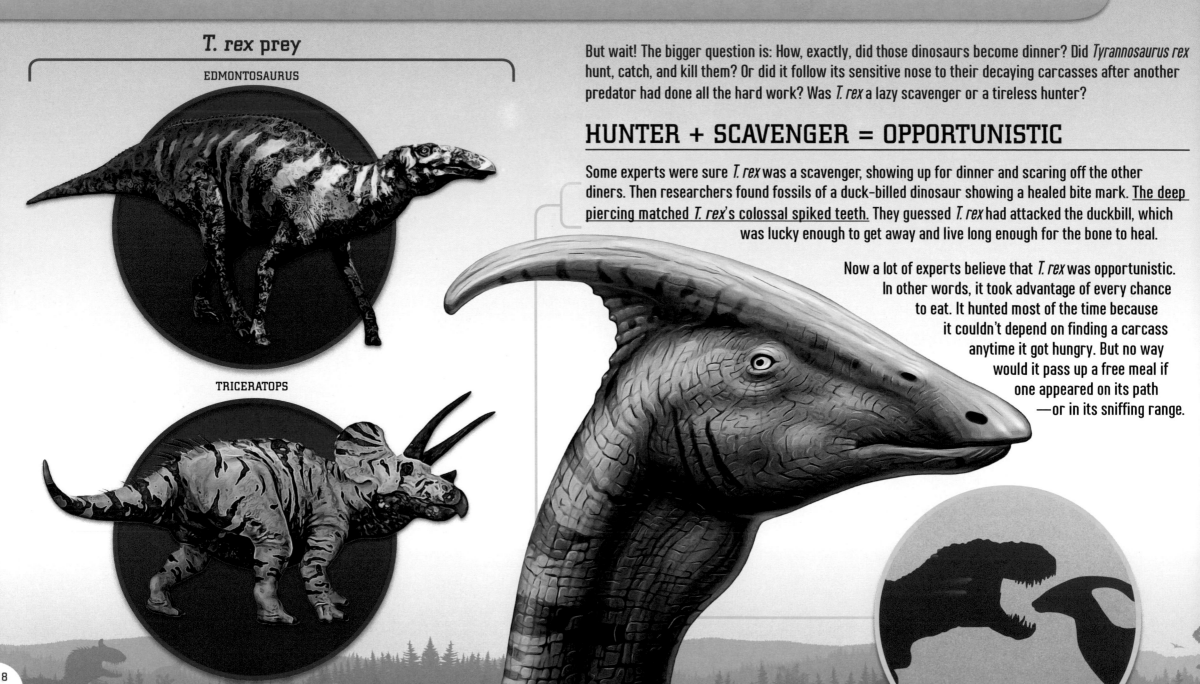

But wait! The bigger question is: How, exactly, did those dinosaurs become dinner? Did *Tyrannosaurus rex* hunt, catch, and kill them? Or did it follow its sensitive nose to their decaying carcasses after another predator had done all the hard work? Was *T. rex* a lazy scavenger or a tireless hunter?

HUNTER + SCAVENGER = OPPORTUNISTIC

Some experts were sure *T. rex* was a scavenger, showing up for dinner and scaring off the other diners. Then researchers found fossils of a duck-billed dinosaur showing a healed bite mark. The deep piercing matched *T. rex*'s colossal spiked teeth. They guessed *T. rex* had attacked the duckbill, which was lucky enough to get away and live long enough for the bone to heal.

Now a lot of experts believe that *T. rex* was opportunistic. In other words, it took advantage of every chance to eat. It hunted most of the time because it couldn't depend on finding a carcass anytime it got hungry. But no way would it pass up a free meal if one appeared on its path —or in its sniffing range.

SOMETHING EATING YOU, T. REX?

T. rex was an apex predator, the animal at the very top of the food chain in its time and place. It had no natural predators—that is, as a healthy adult. But baby *Tyrannosauruses* and old, sick, or weak adults were a different story. They could have been fair game for local carnivores such as the *Dakotaraptor* [duh-COAT-uh-rap-ter], one of the biggest and fiercest predators in *T. rex*'s habitat.

The winged *Dakotaraptor* was too heavy to fly, but it could run faster than *T. rex*. It had claws the size of a human hand. And to add to its hunting advantages, it might have hunted in packs, like other raptors.

Other predators could have been crocodilians, mammals, and birds—and maybe members of its own family. *Tyrannosauruses* could have been cannibals under the right circumstances, such as eating a family member that had died of natural causes. Or one *T. rex* could have eaten another after killing it in a fight for territory or a mate.

Again, they were only following the first rule of nature: <u>EAT.</u>

MEET T. REX'S FEROCIOUS FAMILY

Speaking of family, *Tyrannosaurus rex* had some interesting relatives.

SMALL AND SMART AT THE START

T. rex was part of the *tyrannosauroid* family, which started out small. Tyrannosaurs that lived in the middle-Jurassic period about 170 million years ago were somewhere between the size of a human and a horse. They were too small to be apex predators, but they were intelligent. They had well-developed brains—for dinosaurs—and excellent senses of hearing and smell.

Some experts say that the smart brains of early tyrannosaurs gave later, bigger ones, especially *T. rex*, the mental skills to rise to the top of the food chain. Here are some of *T. rex*'s kin, some of which were apex predators in their own habitats and time periods.

Guanlong [GWAN-long]

This early tyrannosaur lived in China during the late Jurassic period. Its name means "crowned dragon" in Chinese and refers to the crest on its skull, which scientists think may have helped attract mates. It had three fingers on each hand, one more than *T. rex*. *Guanlong* may have sported a full feather covering.

Proceratosaurus [pro-SAIR-uh-toe-SORE-us]

Proceratosaurus lived in Britain in the middle Jurassic period. It was only six feet (1.8 m) long, about the height of an adult human. Like *Guanlong*, it had a crest on the tip of its snout.

Tarbosaurus [TAR-buh-sore-us]

Many call *Tarbosaurus* the Asian *T. rex*. It was about the same gigantic size, and it also had odd, short arms. In fact, its arms were even smaller than *T. rex*'s. *Tarbosaurus* lived in Mongolia 65—70 million years ago, in the late Cretaceous period—about the same time as *Tyrannosaurus rex*.

Albertosaurus [al-BURT-uh-sore-us]

This *T. rex* relative was smaller than its famous cousin but still big by most standards. It was about 30 feet (9 m) long and not as heavy, so it could probably run faster than *T. rex*. It lived in approximately the same time period in Canada, the northern edge of *T. rex*'s turf.

Now that you've met the family, turn the page for other fearsome predators from the Mesozoic. They weren't kin, but they were all terrifying in their own distinctive ways.

GIGANOTOSAURUS

GIANT OF THE SOUTH

Giganotosaurus [jig-a-NOT-oh-SORE-us] means "giant southern lizard" in Greek. This apex predator was truly gigantic. It was as long as a tennis court and could weigh up to 14 tons (12,701 kg).

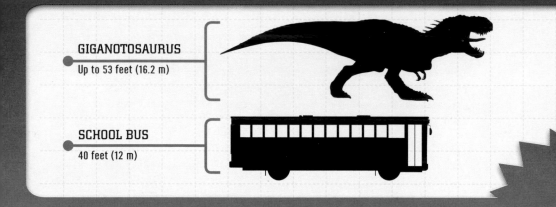

GIGANOTOSAURUS
Up to 53 feet (16.2 m)

SCHOOL BUS
40 feet (12 m)

HEAVYWEIGHT CHAMP

Giganotosaurus lived in Argentina about 97 million years ago, in the late Cretaceous period. It had an absolutely immense body, a head the size of a person, and a mouth full of knife-sharp, sharklike teeth. But for such an enormous creature, it could move pretty quickly.

The first *Giganotosaurus* fossil was found in 1993. It was discovered by Ruben Dario Carolini, an amateur fossil hunter, and was a 70-percent complete skeleton of the massive beast.

FAST FACT

Giganotosaurus weighed as much as 125 full-grown humans.

BITES LIKE A SHARK, RUNS LIKE A DEER.

Giganotosaurus lived in the same geologic time period as *T. rex*, but there is no way these two top predators could have bumped into each other. They were separated not only by two different continents but also by about 30 million years.

If the two had ever met, there would have been a lot more than a bump. There would have been an epic to-the-death battle for dominance between apex predators with the deadliest skills.

GIGANOTOSAURUS VS. T. REX: MONSTER BATTLE

Scientists estimate *Giganotosaurus* could run more than 31 miles per hour (50 kph), which is about the running speed of a white-tailed deer. It's also faster than *T. rex*, whose highest speed estimate is 25 miles per hour (40 kph). *Giganotosaurus*'s thin, pointed tail would have helped it turn corners and change directions more quickly than thick-tailed *T. rex*. It was as much as ten feet (3 m) longer and outweighed *T. rex* by about five tons (4,536 kg).

But . . . *Giganotosaurus*'s arms were even tinier than *T. rex*'s. Its jaws had only about a third of *T. rex*'s bone-crushing power. And in the smarts department, *Giganotorsaurus* would have been outclassed. *T. rex*'s brain was much larger.

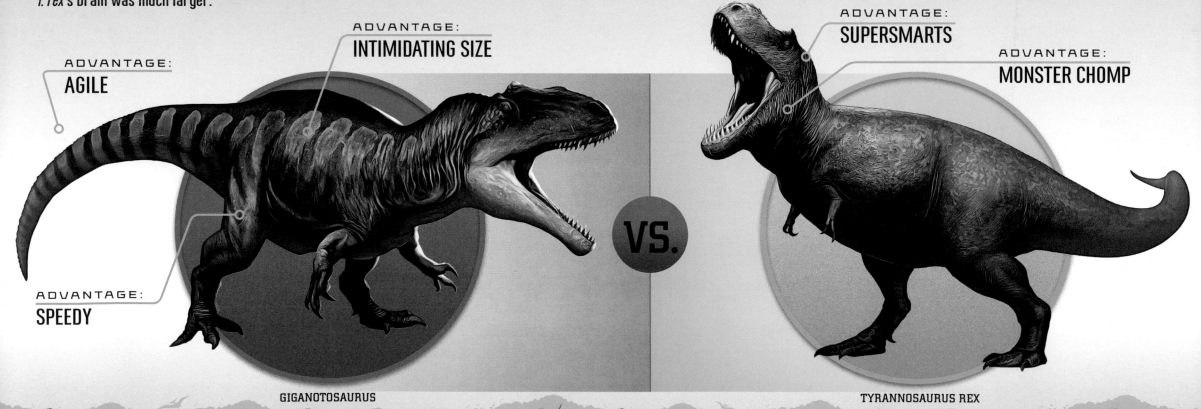

ADVANTAGE:
AGILE

ADVANTAGE:
INTIMIDATING SIZE

ADVANTAGE:
SUPERSMARTS

ADVANTAGE:
MONSTER CHOMP

ADVANTAGE:
SPEEDY

VS.

GIGANOTOSAURUS

TYRANNOSAURUS REX

GREAT WHITE BITE

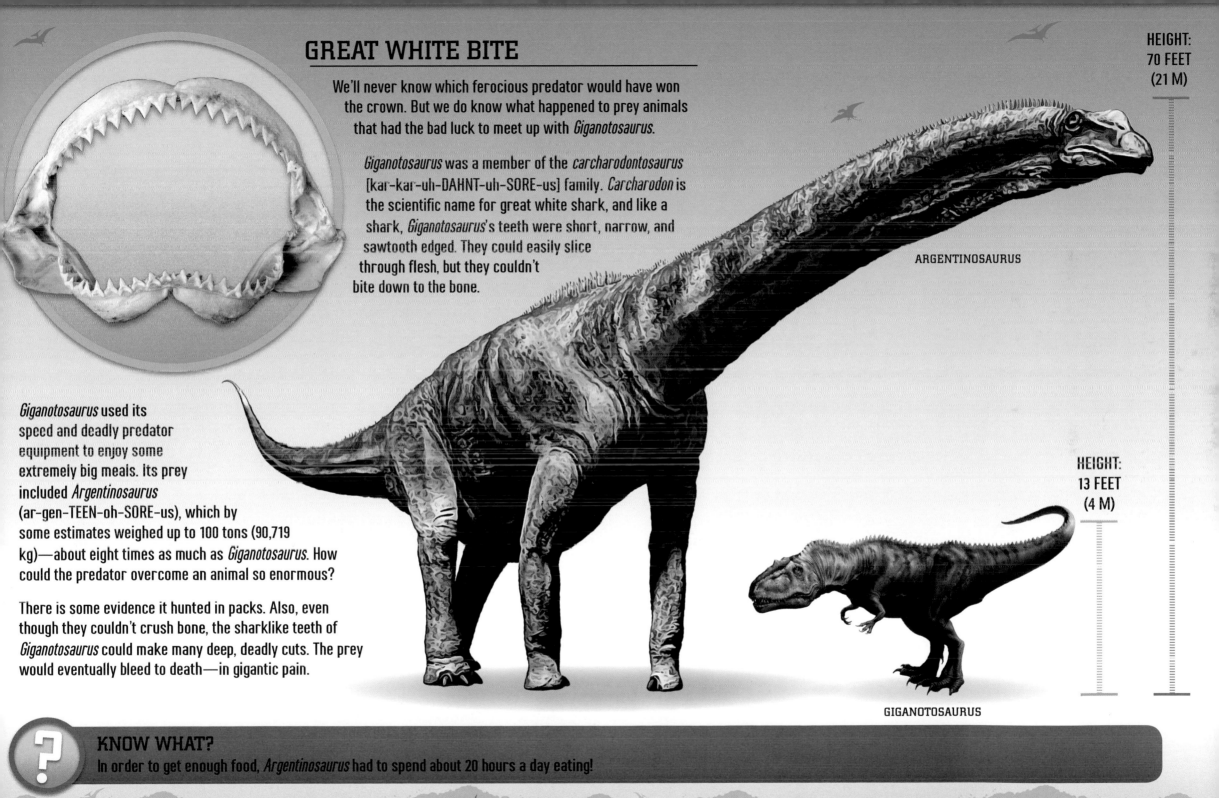

We'll never know which ferocious predator would have won the crown. But we do know what happened to prey animals that had the bad luck to meet up with *Giganotosaurus*.

Giganotosaurus was a member of the *carcharodontosaurus* [kar-kar-uh-DAHNT-uh-SORE-us] family. *Carcharodon* is the scientific name for great white shark, and like a shark, *Giganotosaurus*'s teeth were short, narrow, and sawtooth edged. They could easily slice through flesh, but they couldn't bite down to the bone.

Giganotosaurus used its speed and deadly predator equipment to enjoy some extremely big meals. Its prey included *Argentinosaurus* (ar-gen-TEEN-oh-SORE-us), which by some estimates weighed up to 100 tons (90,719 kg)—about eight times as much as *Giganotosaurus*. How could the predator overcome an animal so enormous?

There is some evidence it hunted in packs. Also, even though they couldn't crush bone, the sharklike teeth of *Giganotosaurus* could make many deep, deadly cuts. The prey would eventually bleed to death—in gigantic pain.

HEIGHT: 70 FEET (21 M)

ARGENTINOSAURUS

HEIGHT: 13 FEET (4 M)

GIGANOTOSAURUS

? KNOW WHAT?

In order to get enough food, *Argentinosaurus* had to spend about 20 hours a day eating!

SPINOSAURUS

SPINE LIZARD

Spinosaurus [SPINE-oh-SORE-us] breaks all records, big time. It was the largest meat-eating dinosaur that ever lived. It was the largest land predator *of any kind* that ever lived. And it was the first swimming dinosaur discovered.

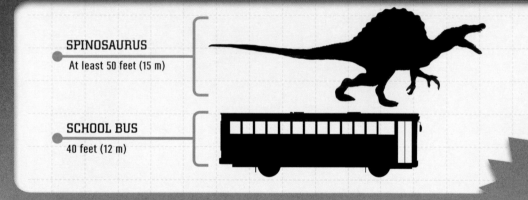

SPINOSAURUS
At least 50 feet (15 m)

SCHOOL BUS
40 feet (12 m)

SAIL AWAY (FAR AWAY, PLEASE)

Spinosaurus lived 112—95 million years ago in North Africa. Scientists estimate it could have been 50 feet (15 m) long and 23 feet (7 m) tall. (Picture five cars parked nose to end with other cars stacked on top of them as high as a three-story building.) Its back was studded with bony spines as tall as a man, covered with skin to form a sail.

FAST FACT

Spinosaurus could weigh up to 20 tons (18,144 kg)—as much as two African elephants.

IMIBLE TROUBLE

The first *Spinosaurus* fossils were discovered by German scientist Ernst Stromer around 1912 and placed in a museum in Germany. They were destroyed when the building was bombed during World War II, but Stromer had made detailed sketches. Based on those sketches and bones found later, scientists suspected *Spinosaurus* spent a lot of time in the water.

It had nostrils near the top of its head, like a crocodile, so it could breathe while hiding just below the surface.

It had a long snout to poke way down in the water for food.

It had teeth like needles to skewer fish in place and then slice and dice.

It had strong jaws to snag and hold slippery fish.

In 2012, a more complete skeleton showed that *Spinosaurus* had solid, dense bones, like penguins and early whales, which would help it stay under water. Land predators had hollow bones for increased oxygen flow and lighter weight, so they could chase their prey faster. Experts now think *Spinosaurus* lived and hunted both on land and in rivers and waterways, making it a double danger.

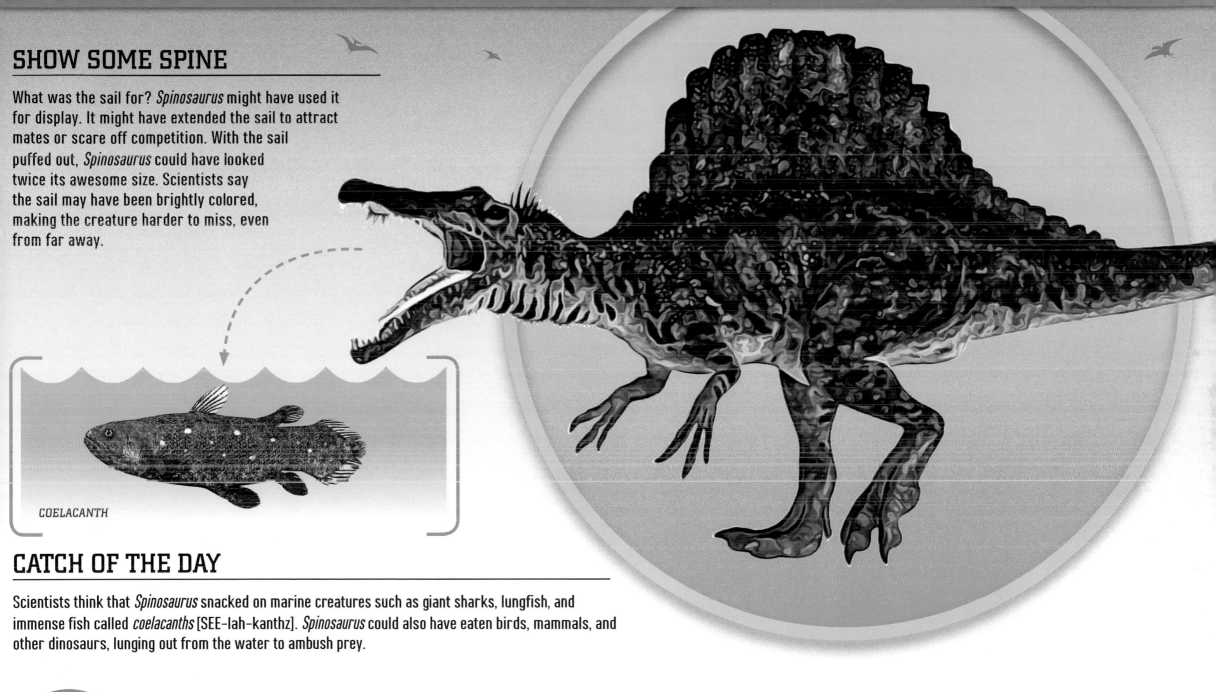

SHOW SOME SPINE

What was the sail for? *Spinosaurus* might have used it for display. It might have extended the sail to attract mates or scare off competition. With the sail puffed out, *Spinosaurus* could have looked twice its awesome size. Scientists say the sail may have been brightly colored, making the creature harder to miss, even from far away.

COELACANTH

CATCH OF THE DAY

Scientists think that *Spinosaurus* snacked on marine creatures such as giant sharks, lungfish, and immense fish called *coelacanths* [SEE-lah-kanthz]. *Spinosaurus* could also have eaten birds, mammals, and other dinosaurs, lunging out from the water to ambush prey.

? KNOW WHAT?

Nobody really knows what color dinosaurs were. Fossilized skin turns gray, like stone. But now scientists have found color pigment from mammal fossils using powerful microscopes. This and other research could help us learn what colors truly were in the prehistoric animal landscape.

ALLOSAURUS

DIFFERENT LIZARD

Scientists gave *Allosaurus* [AL-oh-sore-us] its name, which means "different lizard," because of the unusual hourglass shape of the bones in its spine. This famous megapredator lived in the late Jurassic period, 155–150 million years ago.

The first *Allosaurus* fossils were found in 1877. By 2017, there had been at least 150 fossils discovered, more than any other dinosaur to date. Most fossils were found in Utah, Wyoming, and Colorado, but some were found as far away as Portugal.

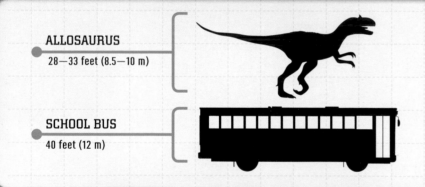

ALLOSAURUS
28—33 feet (8.5—10 m)

SCHOOL BUS
40 feet (12 m)

LIGHTWEIGHT T. REX LOOKALIKE

Despite its name, *Allosaurus* didn't look all that different from *Tyrannosaurus rex*. It was smaller and lighter, which made it faster and more mobile. Like *T. rex*, it had short arms, lots of sharp teeth and powerful legs. Unlike *T. rex*, though, its jaw lacked the power to deliver a killer, bone-crushing bite.

FAST FACT

Allosaurus was smaller than *T. rex*, but, even so, it is the fifth-largest known meat-eating dinosaur. It weighed two to five tons (1,814—4,536 kg).

YIKES!

HEY, BIG AL, YOU'VE GOT A BIG MOUTH!

Scientists have discovered more than 4,000 fossils from many different dinosaur species at or around the world-famous Howe Dinosaur Quarry near Shell, Wyoming. The fossils include two *Allosaurus* skeletons named Big Al and Big Al Two. These nearly complete skeletons tell us a lot about how the real Big Als lived.

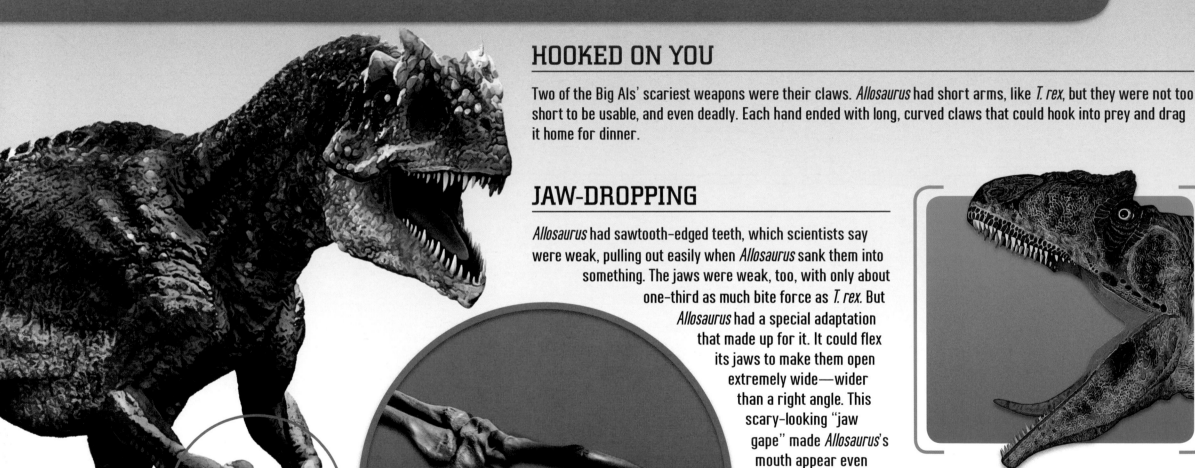

HOOKED ON YOU

Two of the Big Als' scariest weapons were their claws. *Allosaurus* had short arms, like *T. rex*, but they were not too short to be usable, and even deadly. Each hand ended with long, curved claws that could hook into prey and drag it home for dinner.

JAW-DROPPING

Allosaurus had sawtooth-edged teeth, which scientists say were weak, pulling out easily when *Allosaurus* sank them into something. The jaws were weak, too, with only about one-third as much bite force as *T. rex*. But *Allosaurus* had a special adaptation that made up for it. It could flex its jaws to make them open extremely wide—wider than a right angle. This scary-looking "jaw gape" made *Allosaurus*'s mouth appear even bigger than *T. rex*'s.

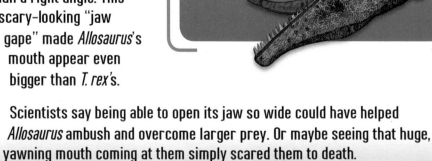

Scientists say being able to open its jaw so wide could have helped *Allosaurus* ambush and overcome larger prey. Or maybe seeing that huge, yawning mouth coming at them simply scared them to death.

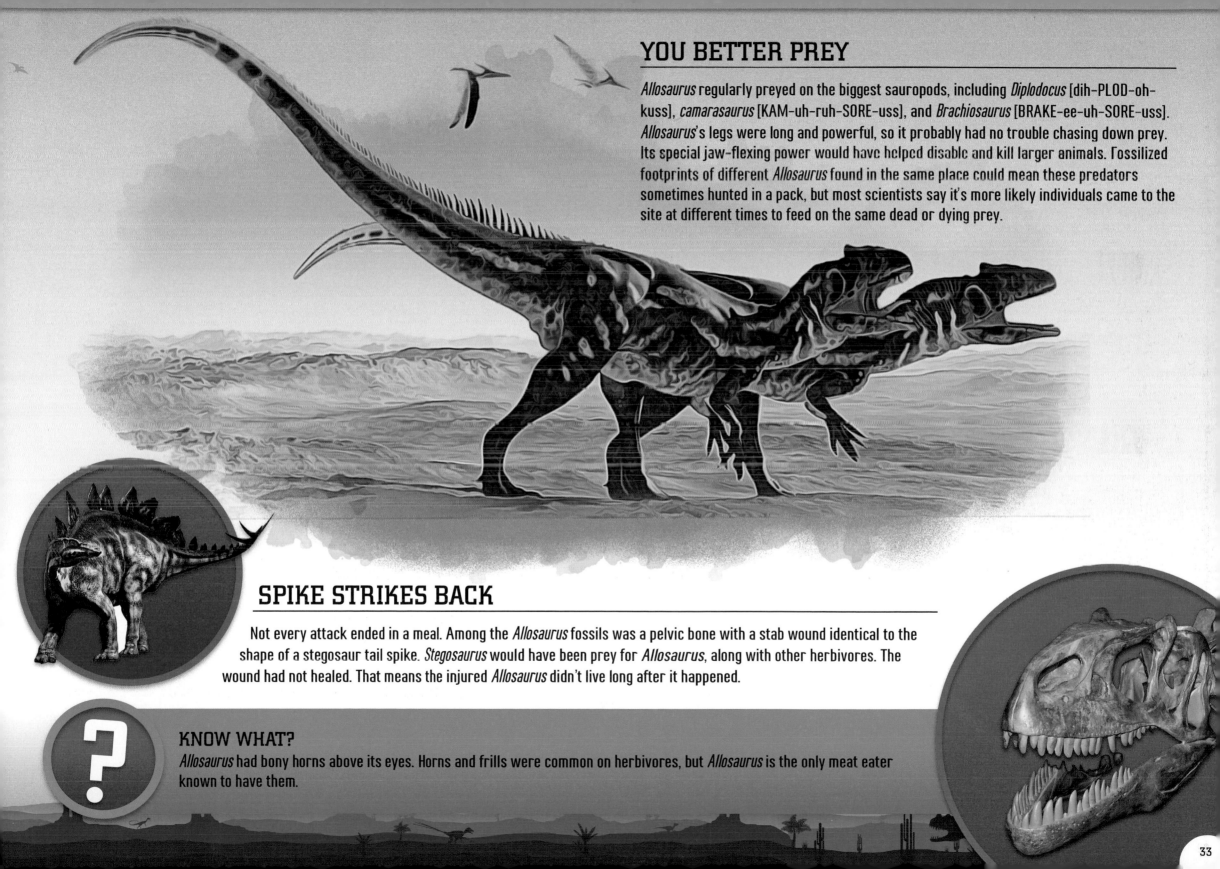

YOU BETTER PREY

Allosaurus regularly preyed on the biggest sauropods, including *Diplodocus* [dih-PLOD-oh-kuss], *camarasaurus* [KAM-uh-ruh-SORE-uss], and *Brachiosaurus* [BRAKE-ee-uh-SORE-uss]. *Allosaurus*'s legs were long and powerful, so it probably had no trouble chasing down prey. Its special jaw-flexing power would have helped disable and kill larger animals. Fossilized footprints of different *Allosaurus* found in the same place could mean these predators sometimes hunted in a pack, but most scientists say it's more likely individuals came to the site at different times to feed on the same dead or dying prey.

SPIKE STRIKES BACK

Not every attack ended in a meal. Among the *Allosaurus* fossils was a pelvic bone with a stab wound identical to the shape of a stegosaur tail spike. *Stegosaurus* would have been prey for *Allosaurus*, along with other herbivores. The wound had not healed. That means the injured *Allosaurus* didn't live long after it happened.

? KNOW WHAT?

Allosaurus had bony horns above its eyes. Horns and frills were common on herbivores, but *Allosaurus* is the only meat eater known to have them.

UTAHRAPTOR

ROBBER FROM UTAH

Guess where most *Utahraptor* [YOU-tah-rap-ter] fossils have been found! You got it—the State of Utah. This quick hunter from the American Southwest was the biggest member of the Dromaeosaur [droe-MAY-uh-sore] family, which are often called raptors.

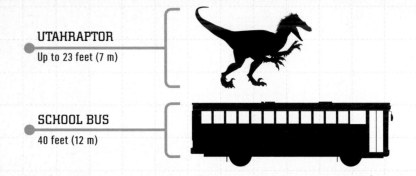

UTAHRAPTOR
Up to 23 feet (7 m)

SCHOOL BUS
40 feet (12 m)

CAPTAIN HOOK

Utahraptor lived about 125 million years ago, in the early Cretaceous period. It had big eyes and long hands, but its feet held the real killing power. Each second toe ended in a sharp hooked claw that was the raptor family trademark. Scientists say that like other dromaeosaurs, *Utahraptor* was almost definitely feathered.

Likely prey for *Utahraptors* would have been iguanodonts (ig-WAN-oh-dahnts), ankylosaurs [an-KYE-low-sores], and duck-billed dinosaurs, or hadrosaurs (HAY-droe-sores).

FAST FACT

One fossilized *Utahraptor* claw measured 9 inches (23 cm).

A FAMILY FOR THE BIRDS

Utahraptor and other dromaeosaurs were not large, but they were some of the fiercest dinosaurs in the Mesozoic. Their most dangerous built-in predatory tool was a razor-sharp hooked claw on the second toe, which could cut long gashes into victims. The toe claw could be retracted when they ran, keeping it undamaged and viciously sharp.

Utahraptor was the largest dromaeosaur. It weighed about half a ton (454 kg), a little more than a grizzly bear. Like other raptors, it had long arms that it kept folded up close to its body when it wasn't hunting and unfolded to strike out at prey. It didn't fly, but it could leap swiftly on prey and dodge away from trouble.

FEATHERED FRIENDS

Dromaeosaurs are the direct dinosaur link to birds. Although no feathered dromaeosaur fossils have been found, scientists did find a Velociraptor arm bone with bumps in the skin to which feathers would have been attached. This is why they think Utahraptor had feathers, too.

KNOW WHAT?

Velociraptor, the cunning hunter from the Jurassic Park movies, is the modern star of the dromaeosaur family. But the supersmart, man-sized predator on the screen is very different from the creature that actually walked the earth. The real Velociraptor was the size of a turkey, with the intelligence of an ostrich. The Jurassic Park Velociraptor was modeled on Deinonychus (dye-NON-ik-us), a large dromaeosaur. The pumped-up brain power was a creative touch, added for extra scariness.

UTAHRAPTOR

VELOCIRAPTOR

STUCK TOGETHER FOREVER IN A PREDATOR TRAP

Raptors were smaller than some of their prey, so scientists think they may have lived and hunted together. In 2001, a team uncovered bones from a group of *Utahraptors* stacked together in a block of sandstone in Utah. Packed in with them were plant-eating iguanodonts .

From these clues, scientists tried to turn back millions of years and figure out what happened. First, they decided the sandstone had been quicksand—thick muck that sucked victims in. Then they came up with two possible theories:

1. The iguanodonts fell into the quicksand. As they struggled to escape, the *Utahraptors* followed their distressed calls and leaped in for an easy meal.

2. The iguanodonts fell into the quicksand and died. Days later, the smell of their decaying carcasses attracted the *Utahraptors*.

More study may give scientists more clues about whether *Utahraptors* hunted in a group, or whether individual predators came upon the trapped iguanodonts one by one.

IGUANODONT GETS TRAPPED
AND CALLS OUT

UTAHRAPTOR FOLLOWS
DISTRESS CALL

UTAHRAPTOR FINDS TRAPPED
IGUANODONT FOR AN EASY KILL

IGUANODONTS DECAYING IN
QUICKSAND

UTAHRAPTOR FOLLOWS ITS
NOSE TO THE SOURCE

UTAHRAPTOR GETS TRAPPED
IN QUICKSAND

HAWK

KNOW WHAT?
Today, "raptor" means a bird of prey—a bird that hunts for food from the air. Modern raptors include birds of prey such as vultures, eagles, hawks, falcons, and condors.

SARCOSUCHUS

FLESH CROCODILE

Sarcosuchus [sar-coe-SOO-cuss] looked like a modern crocodile. Except it was close to twice as long. And about ten times as heavy. Its name, "Flesh Crocodile," comes from its favorite food: raw meat.

SARCOSUCHUS
38—40 feet (11.6—12 m)

SCHOOL BUS
40 feet (12 m)

BREAKNECK BITE

Sarcosuchus lived 112 million years ago, in the early Cretaceous period. Its habitat was North Africa, in an area that is now desert but was once a lush tropical rainforest.

Sarcosuchus was not a dinosaur, but large dinosaurs were its competitors and small ones were its prey. Experts say its super powerful bite could have broken the neck of even the massive *Spinosaurus*, which inhabited the same area at the same time.

FAST FACT

Sarcosuchus could weigh up to ten tons (9,072 kg), about the same as one African elephant. It kept growing its entire life.

SUPERCROC

When a team of researchers digging at a site in Niger, Africa, turned up gigantic crocodile vertebrae, limbs, armor plates, jaws, and a skull, they came up with a nickname for the creature the fossils belonged to: SuperCroc. The fossils were from an especially large *Sarcosuchus*.

HUNTER? AMBUSHER? SCALY SCAVENGER?

Like modern crocodiles, *Sarcosuchus* lived both on land and in the water. It was built to kill in either environment. Its snout was as long as a grown man, and lined with 132 sharp teeth—twice as many as *T. rex*. SuperCroc had a super strong bite, too. It could easily crush fish and large land animals, including big meat-eating dinosaurs. In fact, it would have had an advantage over those towering two-legged creatures: its short legs and low center of gravity would make it hard to push over in a battle.

Although *Sarcosuchus* was likely an adept hunter, scientists believe it behaved like other cold-blooded predators and hid in the water, ambushing its prey in a surprise attack. It also likely scavenged the leftovers of other predator kills.

DID SUPERCROC DO THE DEATH ROLL?

When *Sarcosuchus* snagged a live animal, what did it do with its prey? Modern crocodiles use a move called a death roll. They drag prey into the water and roll over and over with the animal gripped in their jaws until it drowns. Then, while still gripping, they spin their whole bodies to rip off pieces they can swallow.

Scientists say that some ancient crocodiles probably used the death roll, too. However, the ferocious force of the movement creates huge stresses on a crocodile's skull. After studying a model of *Sarcosuchus*'s narrow-snouted skull, researchers now think it did not use the deadly move. The death roll would have been easier for smaller crocodiles. Their lighter weight would have made it easier to spin. SuperCroc possibly took sideways bites or swallowed small prey whole.

CROCODILES HAVE SHRUNK

Sarcosuchus could reach about 38 feet (11.5 m) long and weigh almost 9 tons (8,165 kg). Another ancient crocodile, *Deinosuchus* [DIE-nuh-soo-kuss], could reach a length of 39 feet (11.9 m) and weigh more than 9 tons (8,165 kg). By contrast, the largest reptile alive today, the saltwater crocodile, can grow to only 23 feet (7 m) in length and weigh about a ton.

SARCOSUCHUS

SALTWATER CROCODILE

T. rex and every other giant dinosaur vanished from Earth almost 66 million years ago. In all, 70 percent of species were wiped out, including every land animal larger than a dog. What ended the Age of Dinosaurs?

THE END OF THE MESOZOIC ERA

Scientists know that around that time, an asteroid or comet at least six miles (10 km) wide smashed into the north coast of the Yucatán Peninsula in Mexico, near a place that is now the town of Chicxulub. It caused an explosion two million times more powerful than the biggest known nuclear bomb.

At one point scientists thought the Chicxulub disaster was the sole cause of the mass extinction. But there had been widespread volcanic explosions in India for thousands of years before Chicxulub. The explosions sent dark, poisonous clouds of gases into the air, causing climate change and killing plant life. Survival would have been impossible for many species. Numerous experts now agree that the space rock collision was the last straw in a catastrophe that had already started.

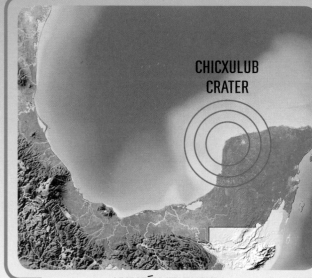

CHICXULUB CRATER

YUCATÁN PENINSULA

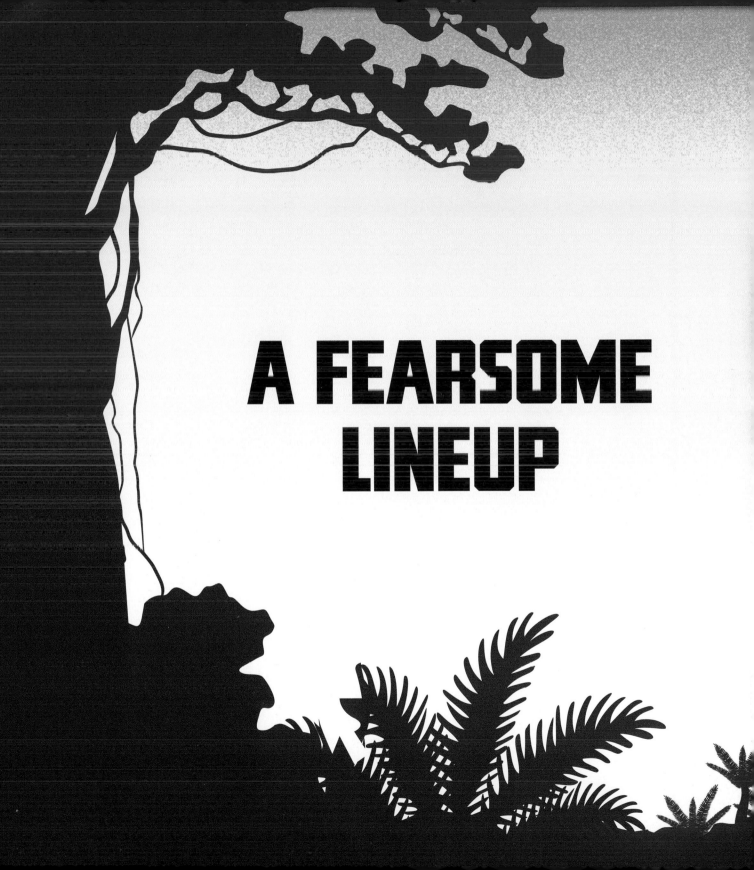

A FEARSOME
LINEUP

ALLOSAURUS
PERIOD: Late Jurassic
LENGTH: 28—33 feet (8.5—10 m)

SARCOSUCHUS
PERIOD: Early Cretaceous
LENGTH: 38—40 feet (11.6—12 m)

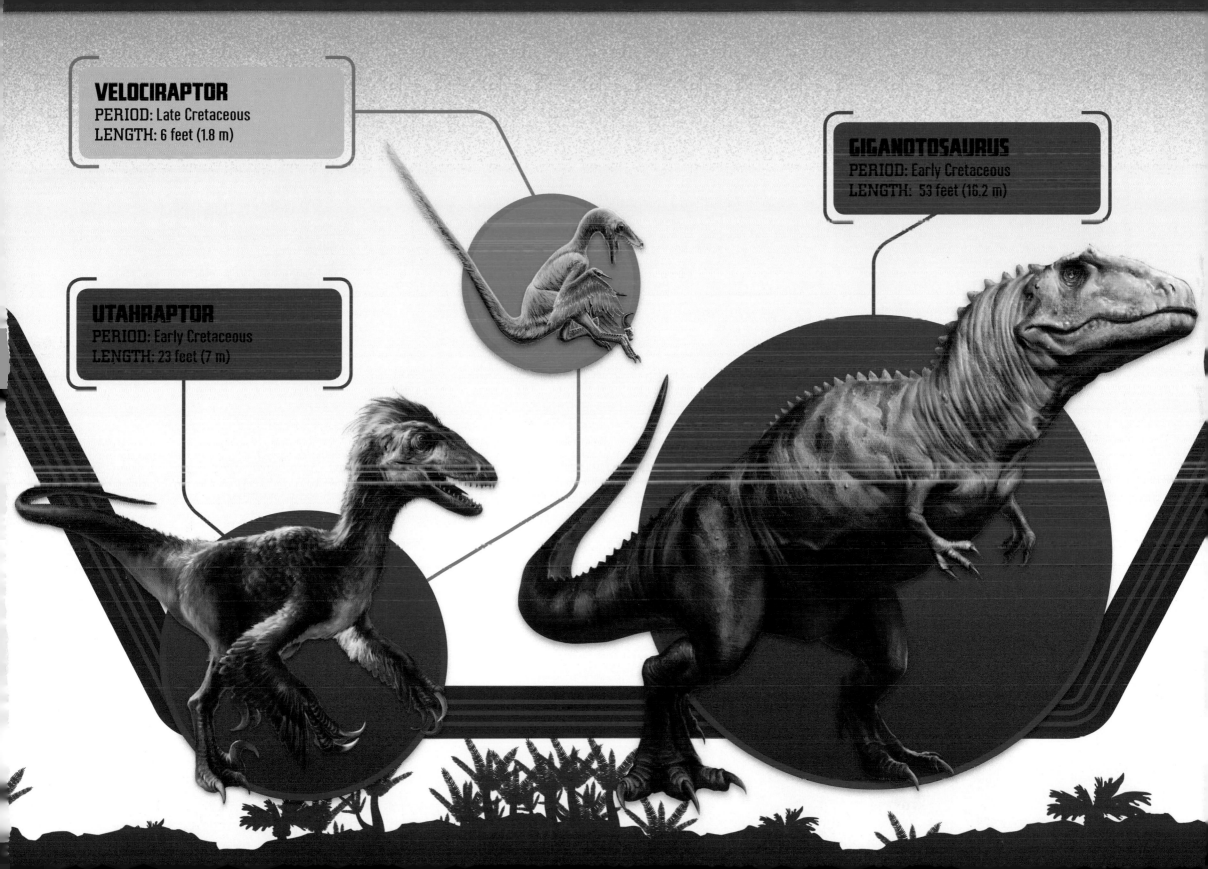

VELOCIRAPTOR
PERIOD: Late Cretaceous
LENGTH: 6 feet (1.8 m)

UTAHRAPTOR
PERIOD: Early Cretaceous
LENGTH: 23 feet (7 m)

GIGANOTOSAURUS
PERIOD: Early Cretaceous
LENGTH: 53 feet (16.2 m)

FLIGHT TO SURVIVAL

Most scientists agree on something else: The dinosaurs did not all die. Some live on today as birds. They are the direct descendants of theropods, the meat-eating group of dinosaurs that included massive predators such as *T. rex*. Specifically, they descend from the dromaeosaur, or raptor, family of theropods.

Knowing the connection, scientists apply what they know about birds to understand dinosaurs better. In one study of a 68-million-year- old dinosaur fossil, they found a chemical that female birds create when they are carrying eggs or have recently laid them. The chemical makes calcium for stronger eggshells. Scientists guessed that if bird eggs needed the chemical, so did dinosaur eggs. So they think this dinosaur was a female. Before this study, there was no reliable way to tell a dinosaur's sex.

UTAHRAPTOR

EAGLE

REPTILE RELATIVES

Crocodiles, lizards, turtles, and snakes are also modern dinosaur relatives, but not direct descendants. Dinosaurs belonged to a large group called archosaurs, which means "ruling reptiles." At the very beginning of the Mesozoic Era, about 250 million years ago, the group broke into two branches: crocodilians in one and another that includes dinosaurs, pterosaurs, and birds.

KNOW WHAT?
Archaeopteryx (are-key-OP-ter-ichs) is the earliest known bird. It evolved from raptor-type dinosaurs in the late Jurassic period, about 150 million years ago. *Archaeopteryx* was the size of a pigeon and had a fully feathered tail and wings. It had raptor-like claws on its hand and jaws with teeth instead of a beak.

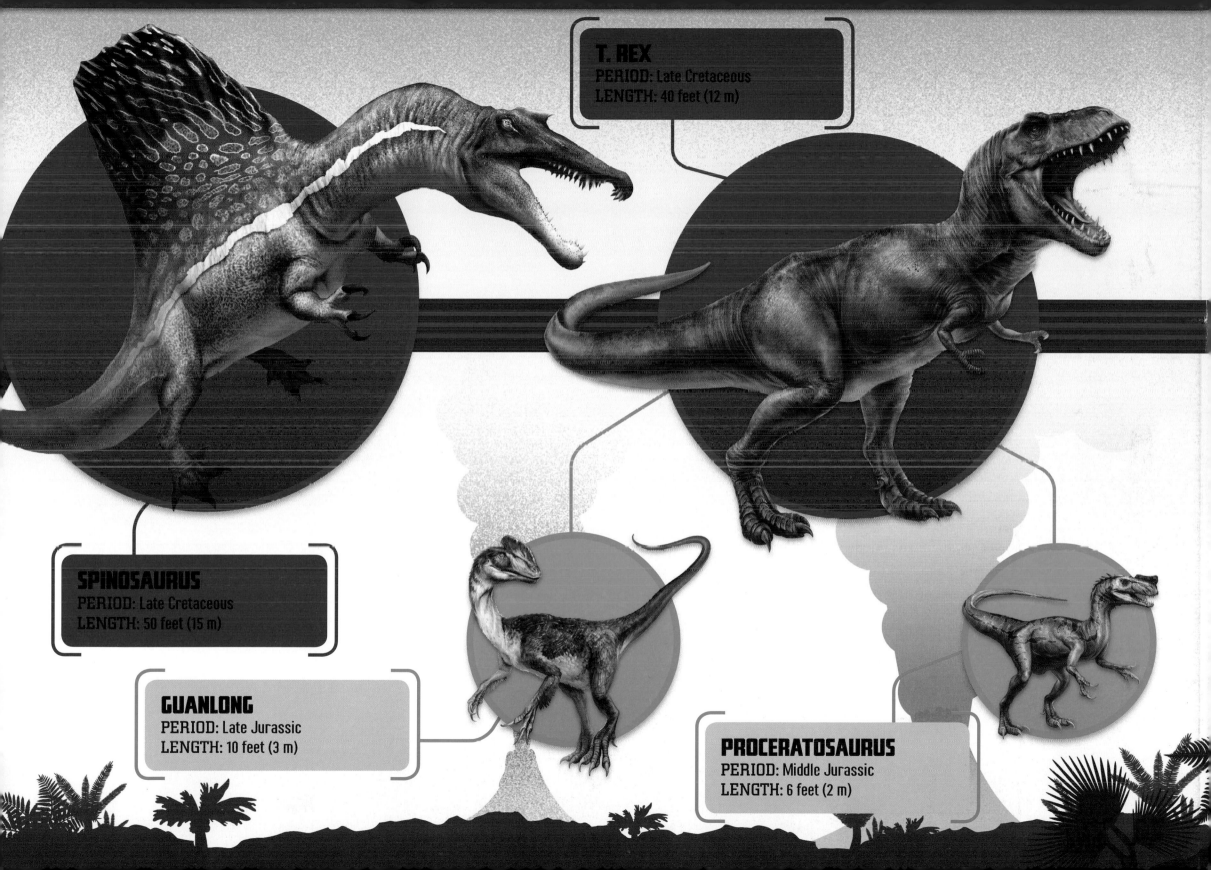

T. REX
PERIOD: Late Cretaceous
LENGTH: 40 feet (12 m)

SPINOSAURUS
PERIOD: Late Cretaceous
LENGTH: 50 feet (15 m)

GUANLONG
PERIOD: Late Jurassic
LENGTH: 10 feet (3 m)

PROCERATOSAURUS
PERIOD: Middle Jurassic
LENGTH: 6 feet (2 m)

GLOSSARY

Apex predator
Animal with no natural predators within its time and place

Archosaurs
Dominant reptiles in the Triassic period, including dinosaurs, pterosaurs, and crocodiles

Asteroid
A large space rock

Carnivore
Animal that eats other animals

Climate
Weather conditions of an area, including rain and snow, humidity, winds, and temperature

Cold-blooded
Having blood whose temperature changes with the environment

Comet
Ball of rock, ice, and dust traveling through space

Coprolites
Fossilized poop

Cretaceous
The third geologic time period in the Mesozoic Era, from 145 to 66 million years ago

Crocodilian
Member of a group of reptiles that includes crocodiles, alligators, and their ancient relatives

Curator
Person in charge of a museum or art collection

Descendant
Species that evolved from an earlier species

Dromaeosaurs
Family of carnivorous dinosaurs scientists think are the direct ancestors of birds. Also called raptors.

Ecosystem
A community of interconnected living and nonliving things

Environment
The natural surroundings in which an animal or plant lives

Era
A very long unit of time divided into shorter units called periods

Evolve
To change over many years

Extinction
The death of all members of a species

Fossils
Preserved body parts or traces of an animal or plant

Gondwana
The southern supercontinent during the Jurassic period

Habitat
Place where a plant or animal lives naturally

Hadrosaur
Plant-eating dinosaur, also known as a duckbill

Herbivore
Animal that eats plants

Iguanodont
Large, plant-eating dinosaur common in the early Cretaceous

Jaw gape
The widest angle an animal can open its mouth

Jurassic
The second of three geologic time periods in the Mesozoic Era, from 200 to 145 million years ago

Laurasia
The northern supercontinent during the Jurassic period

Mammal
Type of warm-blooded vertebrate that feeds its newborn young with milk

Marine
Relating to the ocean or sea

Mass extinction
The disappearance of many species due to a huge disaster

Mesozoic
The era known as the Age of Dinosaurs, from 251 to 66 million years ago

Omnivore
Animal that eats both plants and other animals

Paleontologist
Scientist who studies fossils to learn about the history of plant and animal life on Earth

Pangaea
The supercontinent that included all the land in the world during the early Mesozoic Era

Period
A unit of time millions of years long

Plesiosaurs
A group of prehistoric marine reptiles, many with long necks

Pterosaurs
Flying reptiles, some huge, with wings of stretched skin that lived during the Mesozoic Era

Predator
An animal that hunts and kills other animals for food

Prey
An animal that is hunted and eaten by predators

Sauropod
A type of long-necked plant-eating dinosaur, often enormous

Scavenger
An animal that feeds on decaying matter

Species
A group of animals or plants that are similar and can produce offspring

Spine
A stiff, pointed outgrowth of an animal or plant

Stegosaur
A type of plant-eating dinosaur with plates and spikes

Supercontinent
A single land mass from which multiple continents formed

Theropod
A meat-eating dinosaur that walked on two legs

Triassic
The first of three geologic time periods that make up the Mesozoic Era, from 251 to 200 million years ago

Tyrannosaurs
Meat-eating dinosaurs including and closely related to Tyrannosaurus rex

Vertebrae
Small bones that make up the spine

Warm-blooded
Having blood that does not change with the temperature of the environment

Wingspan
Distance from the tip of one wing to the tip of the other with both wings outstretched

Brimming with creative inspiration, how-to projects, and useful information to enrich your everyday life, Quarto Knows is a favorite destination for those pursuing their interests and passions. Visit our site and dig deeper with our books into your area of interest: Quarto Creates, Quarto Cooks, Quarto Homes, Quarto Lives, Quarto Drives, Quarto Explores, Quarto Gifts, or Quarto Kids.

First published in 2017 by becker&mayer!, an imprint of The Quarto Group, 11120 NE 33rd Place, Suite 201, Bellevue, WA 98004 USA.

www.QuartoKnows.com

becker&mayer! titles are also available at discount for retail, wholesale, promotional, and bulk purchase. For details, contact the Special Sales Manager by email at specialsales@quarto.com or by mail at The Quarto Group, Attn: Special Sales Manager, 401 Second Avenue North, Suite 310, Minneapolis, MN 55401 USA.

17 18 19 20 21   5 4 3 2 1

ISBN: 978-0-7603-5983-9

Library of Congress Cataloging-in-Publication Data is available.

Author: Jacqueline Ball
Design: Sam Dawson
Editorial: Ashley McPhee
Production: Tom Miller
Product Development: Blake Mitchum

Printed, manufactured, and assembled in Shenzhen, China, 10/17

Image credits (Images used throughout):
Nine silhouettes of dinosaurs © SiuWing/ Shutterstock; tooth from a Spinosaurid dinosau © Ryan M. Bolton/ Shutterstock; Mexico © AridOcean/ Shutterstock; green iguana eye © Enrique Ramos/ Shutterstock; golden eagle © withGod/ Shutterstock; Dinosaurs silhouettes © Meletios/ Shutterstock; Internal organs © Sedova Elena/ Shutterstock; vector tropical rainforest © SaveJungle/ Shutterstock; dinosaur © Viktorya170377/ Shutterstock; crocodile skull © Nagel Photography/ Shutterstock; Vector horizontal banner © Vertyr/ Shutterstock; Shark Jaw Bone © Seashell World/ Shutterstock; Red-tailed Hawk © Le Do/ Shutterstock; vector film strip © Drawbot/ Shutterstock; Vector silhouette of a people working © majivecka/ Shutterstock; Continental drift on the planet Earth © Designua/ Shutterstock; Allosaurus on Mountain © Catmando/ Shutterstock; Allosaurus Skeleton © Steve Bower/ Shutterstock; vector evening in jungle © SaveJungle/ Shutterstock; Saurophaganax © Herschel Hoffmeyer/ Shutterstock; man holding his nose © Tribalium/ Shutterstock; American alligator © Valentyna Chukhlyebova/ Shutterstock; 3D digital render of a dinosaur Spinosaurus © Valentyna Chukhlyebova/ Shutterstock; Hooded vulture © Eric Isselee/ Shutterstock; Rattlesnake © IrinaK/ Shutterstock; Dinosaur spinosaurus © Miceking/ Shutterstock; Spinosaurus 3D render © Herschel Hoffmeyer/ Shutterstock; Utahraptor 3D render © Herschel Hoffmeyer/ Shutterstock; Melon © sarawutnirothon/ Shutterstock; Silhouette of eoraptor © wong salam/ Shutterstock; Edmontosaurus 3D illustration © Warpaint/ Shutterstock; 3D rendering of Utahraptor © Herschel Hoffmeyer/ Shutterstock; 3D rendering of Archaeopteryx © Herschel Hoffmeyer/ Shutterstock; 3D rendering of Velociraptor © Herschel Hoffmeyer/ Shutterstock; Stegosaurus 3D illustration © Warpaint/ Shutterstock; 3D rendering of Triceratops © Herschel Hoffmeyer/ Shutterstock; spinosaurus skeleton © Evgeniy Mahnyov/ Shutterstock; 3D rendering of Tyrannosaurus Rex © Herschel Hoffmeyer/ Shutterstock; 3D rendering of Tyrannosaurus Rex © Herschel Hoffmeyer/ Shutterstock; A large Meteor burning and glowing as it hits the earth's atmosphere © solarseven/ Shutterstock; Tyrannosaurus rex dead © sruilk/ Shutterstock; Utahraptor 3D illustration © Warpaint/ Shutterstock; Vector scales Icon © tatianasun/ Shutterstock; Argentinosaurus 3D illustration © Warpaint/ Shutterstock; Desert trip © 32 pixels/ Shutterstock; 3D rendering of Allosaurus © Herschel Hoffmeyer/ Shutterstock; dinosaur silhouettes © Milagli/ Shutterstock; Silhouettes of dinosaurs © Viktorya170377/ Shutterstock

301866

ASSEMBLING THE FOSSILS

1. Start with the neck vertebrae. Insert the post on vertebrae 1 into the neck vertebrae. Then attach the remaining vertebrae (2, 3, 4, 5).

2. Attach the rib cages to vertebrae 1.

3. Piece together the broken leg and attach the hips, legs, arms, and head.

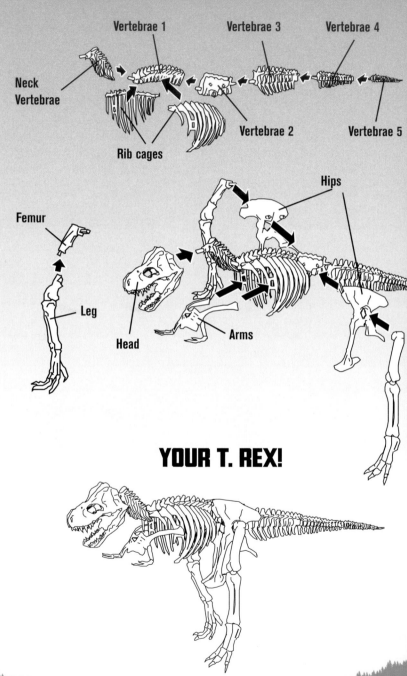

YOUR T. REX!